# Praying Through Addiction

Desiree Kelley

BookLeaf Publishing

India | USA | UK

Presentation by *BookLeaf Publishing*

Web: www.bookleafpub.com

E-mail: info@bookleafpub.com

ISBN: 9789360942779

First edition 2024

# Addiction

Addiction is a powerful force
It takes over your mind and body
It has no remorse
It doesn't care who it hurts along its path
Just don't stand in its way
Or you will feel the wrath
Watching your loved one
Die a little more every day
Praying, wishing, hoping that soon
It will go away
It will make you promises
So you can see them break
It will tell you that it's sorry
That it's sober and awake
Only to show you later
That trusting it was a big mistake
Because addiction is a powerful force
It will take over your mind and body
Without any remorse

# Through the Eyes of an Addict

As my problems
Get bigger and bigger
I pop that pill
And pull the trigger
Everyday I wake up
And play the game
Whether I live or die
My feelings are the same
People will wonder why
As my family is put to shame
I'll give a list of excuses
But it's me to blame
I created this life
Full of turmoil and friction
Because all I care about
Is feeding my addiction

# Breaking the Chains

Holy Spirit fill me
Run through my veins
Until you're all that I see
Take away this fear and doubt
That has creeped its way inside of me
Nervous and scared
Is not how you want us to be
You died on the cross
So that we could be free
Free from these chains
That keep trying to bind me
Telling me a child of God
Is something I'll never be
But I know we can do this
Because you'll be with me
Through every up and down
Every storm in the sea
Jesus you will calm the waves
That stir inside of me
Just the mention of your name
Makes the demons flee
From inside of me
And a child of God
I will be

# Temptations

Anxiety taking over
I don't know what to do
I pray and I pray
And the devil keeps breaking through
Help me God, keep him away
But those thoughts creep in
And I know I can't let them stay
It only opens the door
And turns me away
From the sight of you
So I hit my knees and pray
Lord God take this addiction
Take it all away
Banish those negative thoughts
I give it all to you
Just as you say
Because I know the devil's a liar
And you are the truth, the light, and the way

# Urges

I keep getting these urges
It feels like electricity
Hitting my body in surges
My mind in a war with itself
Asking what matters more
My sanity or my health
One side says
Just go to the store
The other side says
Just trust in God more
He has already done it
He has already won the war
So don't believe the lies
That I will never be nothing more
Than a failure
Walking into that store
Trust in God, my savior
He sent Jesus to set me free
From the lies that Satan
Tells my mind about me

# Let Go

I'm learning to let go
I know that God is the only one
Who will ever really know
What's really to come
And where I will go
I knew I wasn't strong enough
The sin was all around
Trying to bury me
Until I rose out of the ground
I couldn't do it alone
I need my Jesus around
Because he makes me strong
Strong enough to bury the addiction
That I've carried for so long
Eating away at me
Because I knew it was wrong
It was selfish and stupid
I told myself I'll never do it
I told myself I'll never belong
Because my addiction made me weak
But then my Jesus is strong
And reminds me he has been here
Right by my side all along

# Keep Fighting

Just got to keep moving
Keep myself busy
Don't think about it
How hard can that be
Harder than I thought
Oh God, help me
Help me to stay focused
Help me to see
That I don't have to struggle
When you are with me
That it is you who keeps me safe
Through the raging sea
My savior has come
To set me free
And help me to remember
I'm never alone
When God is fighting with me

# My Eyes Are Open

God you are faithful
You never tell a lie
You are there in the good
And you are there when I cry
You take things away
That were killing me inside
All the anger, hatred, resistance
Was thrown to the side
So you could do what you needed
Opening my heart and eyes wide
Wide enough to see
How much I need you in my life
To be a better person
A better mother and wife
Thank you my God
For taking away the strife
Pointing me towards
A much better life

# Focus on the Positive

Lord draw me closer to you
I want to scream it out
Everything that you do
How you took this addiction away
How you give me strength
To keep fighting every day
You are my refuge
And to you I run
You are the destroyer of the dark
The raiser of the sun
With you by my side
I can conquer it all
For when I fall short
You make me tall
And carry me through
With you there is nothing
That I cannot do

# Stay Strong

Today was hard in so many ways
I know God has a plan
But the worst case scenario just plays
Runs through my mind
Leaving my faith in a daze
Trying to distract me from what I need
To feel the holy spirit when I praise
To not feel this heaviness
I know what happens when it stays
I begin to question everything
Falling into the game the devil plays
Messing with my mind
In so many ways
But my God keeps me strong
Through music I give praise
And it's my poetry and scripture
That gets me through the hard days
Because without these the devil runs free
And we all know how he plays
Not very fair
And evil in his ways
I rebuke you devil
Go back where you belong
So I can finish praising my God
Through poetry and song

# Don't Cave In

I'm angry
I'm irritable
I'm happy
I'm sad
I still haven't smoked
And for this
I am glad
Even though I don't show it
Because I seem mad
I'm really trying
To keep it together
I know this change
Is for the better
But how much more
Do I have to weather
Before the storm is clear
And I can sail into the ocean
Without that fear
Fear of failing
A battle you already won
When you sent us Jesus
Your only son
To rescue us from drowning
All glory to the holy one
Because without him
My story would be done

# Wasted

I chose to stay sober
Didn't get wasted
Almost forgot
How good it tasted
Liquid burning
Down on the inside
Shame and guilt
Making me want to hide
As my world crashes
Everything starts to collide
Tearing apart
My ego and pride
Good thing I put that
Desire to the side
Remembering just how bad
That it really tasted
Every single time that
I chose to get wasted

# Help Me

Have you ever felt alone
With people all around
You feel the need to talk
But you never make a sound
People have their own problems
But you want to reach out
You need someone to talk to
But then your mind fills with doubt
Do people really care
What you are sad about
Do they really want you to express it
To get it all out
Or would they rather have the fake version
The one that smiles and says I'm okay
When inside I am fighting myself
To make it through each day
These intrusive thoughts
Never ending in my mind
If you think that I'm okay
Clearly you are blind
I am not okay
I am having a hard time
Is wanting a friend that cares
Truely such a crime
I just want someone

To show me they are kind
And help me fight this addiction
That constantly plagues my mind

# Wide awake

My mind racing
Here we go again
Through the house pacing
Will this ever end
I'm starting to lose sleep
But my mind does not care
My body is feeling weak
All I can do is bear
Stare into the darkness
And hope to get some rest
Tell myself to stop
And hope for the best
The mind is so powerful
It can make you believe so many things
But it is not powerful enough
To tell you what the future brings
So as I lay here
And try to predict my day
I realize these thoughts
Are only getting in my way
I tell them to stop
As people always say
But that's like telling the sun
Not to come up today
Because it is so natural

To do what I do
Even when I know
That it's not good for you
So I tell myself
I can only do what I can do
And hope that tomorrow
I can just make it through

# Internal Battle

Fighting to survive in every way
New obstacles thrown at me
Every single day
Screaming on the inside
Using smiles and jokes
To try to hide
What really lingers
The darkness inside
Ripping me to pieces
Crawling through my vein
Screaming out
My mind in so much pain
Silenced on the outside
No where to run
Pretending to hold it together
Floating around the issues
Like a weighted feather
My insides are scarred
But on the outside I look fine
Faking it can be so hard
As I tell everyone I'm okay
I continue to battle this addiction
Every single day

# They Say

The say addiction is not real
They say that it's fake
Until it leaves the news
And enters your world
Only to take
Take away those we love
Oh, so now you're awake
Now it's real
When it's up in your face
And you have no choice but to deal
As it damages the people you love
But what do I do?
Live in fear?
Pull away to protect those
I hold so dear
Is that really the solution
Total isolation, depression, and fear
I have a solution
That has been proven effective
Over thousands of years
A name that can banish
Anxiety, depression, and fear
A name that can take addiction
And make it disappear
A name that I can call on

Anytime of day
In any type of way
Screaming, crying, or
Singing his praise
His name has stood
Through all of the days
And all of the nights
Jesus is the name I call
For all of my fights

# Overcoming Addiction

My God is bigger than you
Bigger than any addiction
Or struggles I go through
My God can save me
When I don't know what to do
He can guide me
He can heal me through and through
My God is bigger
And he will come through
Addiction can't beat me
As long as I have you
Together we will fight this
Because that's what you do
You go to battle for us
And guide us through
These difficult times
That try to consume you

# Feeling Stuck

Stuck in a situation
My mind is covered in contemplation
What to do or say
Does it really matter anyway?
Life is like a lottery
That I can never win
But every day I wake up
I give it a spin
Hoping today is better
At least better than the last
Wishing that I could change
Everything bad in the past
Maybe one day
I can have that peace of mind
Or the truth of the matters
I will find

# Trying to Hide

There's a part of me inside
A part you'll never see
A part deep down
That will never be free
It's where I hide my sorrow
It's where I hide my pain
It helps me get through
Helps me to maintain
I must keep these parts from coming out
Filling my body and mind with doubt
I must push them down
Deep down inside
Where pain and sorrow
Linger and hide

# Addiction Takes Away

Sometimes I fear I can't go on
My heart rips in two
The longer you're gone
I feel so dead inside without you
I pray one that I you will return to me
Back into my arms forever
But deep down I know you can never
Sometimes I wish I could turn back time
When the world seemed so simple
And you were here in body and mind
I lost everything when you left me here
Alone in this world
Full of fear

# Change the Past

I dreamed of you tonight
While sleeping in my bed
I dreamed we were together
Talking and laughing about what was never said
Like how much I miss you after all of these
years
And how the mention of your name
Still brings me to tears
How I wish these dreams could last
Or that somehow, someway I could change the
past
I wish there was a way
That I could make you stay
So I wouldn't have to lose you
When the night turns into day